1939-1945
WORLD WAR TWO

AUTHOR

Carlo Cucut was born in Nole (TO) in 1955. He cultivated a passion for history as a boy and over the years has deepened this interest by dedicating himself to historical research. He published articles in the italian magazines: "Storia del XX Secolo", "Storie & Battaglie", "Milites" and "Ritterkreuz". He published various volumes for Marvia Edizioni: "Penne Nere on the eastern border. History of the Alpini's Regiment "Tagliamento" 1943-1945 ", winner of the "De Cia" Award; "Attilio Viziano. Memories of a war correspondent "; "Armed Forces of RSI on the eastern front"; "Armed Forces of RSI on the Western Front"; "Armed Forces of RSI on the Gothic Line"; "Alpini in the City of Rijeka 1944-1945". For the Trentino Modeling Group he published "The armed forces of RSI 1943-1945. Land forces ".

PUBLISHING'S NOTES

LICENSES COMMONS

For a complete list of Soldiershop titles please contact Luca Cristini Editore on our website: www.soldiershop.com or www.cristinieditore.com. E-mail: info@soldiershop.com

Title: **THE FINNISH ARMOURED UNITS** Code.: **WTW-028 ENG** By Carlo Cucut ISBN code: 978-88-93277921
First edition November 2021
Text: English 130 images : layout: 7x10 Cover & Art Design: Luca S. Cristini

WITNESS TO WAR (SOLDIERSHOP) is a trademark of Luca Cristini Editore, via Orio, 35/4 - 24050 Zanica (BG) ITALY.

WITNESS TO WAR

THE FINNISH ARMORED UNITS

FROM THE CONSTITUTION TO THE END OF THE SECOND WORLD WAR

PHOTOS & IMAGES FROM WORLD WARTIME ARCHIVES

CARLO CUCUT

CONTENTS

THE FINNISH ARMORED UNITS FROM 1919 TO 1939

Finland, after declaring independence from Russia on December 6, 1917, and being plunged into a painful civil war between the Red Guards and the White Guards which lasted several months, won by the latter with the support of Germany, with the Conference of Paris in 1919 was finally recognized internationally as a Republic. One of the first measures implemented by the new government was the expansion and strengthening program of its army: the Suomen Maavoimat. Based on compulsory conscription, despite a growing economy, he was currently weakly equipped and technically backward. The establishment of an armored department was included among the first projects, destined to be realized. The only vehicles in service at the time were a few Russian armored cars, used by the Red Guards and captured by the White Guards. On July 15, 1919, the Hyökkäysvaunurykmentti, the assault tank regiment, was established on the island of Santahamina, located in the capital Helsinki, a place where small tactical exercises could be carried out and fired with real ammunition. 32 Renault FT Modèle 1917 tanks were then purchased from France, probably the most advanced tank at the time. Arriving in Finland, departing from the French port of Le Havre, in two shipments, the FT-17s were delivered to the Regiment on August 26, 1919. Together with the wagons, 6 Latil TAR TP 1915 tractors with La Buire trailer, 5,000 bullets of 37 were also purchased. mm and 1.2 million 8 mm bullets.

The tanks were newly built, 14 armed with the 37 mm Puteaux SA 18 cannon and 18 with the 8 mm Hotchkiss Mle 1914 machine gun. The Finns called the chariots equipped with cannon koiras (male) and those with the machine gun naaras (female).

Following strong French diplomatic pressure, from 17 October 1919 two tanks had to be loaned to General Judenič's white Russian army, engaged in the offensive for the conquest of St. Petersburg. The offensive failed, the Army under Judenič's command withdrew to Estonia and the two FT-17s remained at his disposal until April 9, 1920. As the two tanks were in poor condition when they were returned, France sent two tanks to replacement in the same month. Thus 34 Renault FT-17 tanks were in service in the Suomen Maavoimat.

Since it was the first armored department, and there were no soldiers with specific experience present, in addition to the supply of tanks, France also took care of the training of personnel, sending a core of military instructors under the command of Captain Pivetau. The recruits were selected from among those who had technical training or experience while the officers came largely from the cavalry.

The Hyökkäysvaunurykmentti was structured as an artillery regiment on two battalions, each of which on three batteries of 2 sections each. Each section consisted of a male and a female Renault, while the battery commander was equipped with a female Renault, for a total of 15 tanks per battalion and 30 tanks, 12 Renault with cannon and 18 with machine gun, for the Regiment.

At the end of 1919 the staff serving in the Hyökkäysvaunurykmentti were:

- Officers = 11
- Non-commissioned officers = 73 (between permanent and conscript military personnel)
- Recruits = 111

Initially, as there were no specific regulations for the armored weapon, the French manuals were translated, then, in the mid-1920s, Colonel Sihvo drafted the "Training Rules for Tanks".

The first public appearance of the Hyökkäysvaunurykmentti was the parade on May 16, 1920, which took place in the capital Helsinki, in front of an attentive and enthusiastic public of the new medium.

The difficult connections with the island of Santahamina created problems for the Regiment, laying the foundations for its transfer to the Poltinaho barracks in Hameenlinna, which took place on 2 September 1921.

The particular orography of the Finnish territory, the extreme climatic conditions, the economic hardships of the period, as well as a distorted view on the use of armored forces on the territory by the High Commands, prevented the development and modernization of the Hyökkäysvaunuryk-mentti, in the meantime renamed Tankkirykmenti, Tank Regiment. In 1925 the unit was reclassi-fied Panssaripataljoona, Armored Battalion, and in 1927 Pansaarikomppania, Armored Company, the latter in the following years only carried out purely training tasks or, as in the period Febru-ary-March 1932, of public order following the revolt of Mäntsälä.

In June 1933, despite the perplexities of the military leaders, the program relating to the replace-ment of the obsolete FT-17 began, proceeding with the purchase of various models to be subjected to tests and comparisons.

The Ministry of Defense ordered three different models of British tanks:
- 1 Vickers 6-Ton (or Vickers Mark E) Type B
- 1 Vickers Carden-Loyd Mk VI B
- 1 Vickers Carden-Loyd M / 1933

Along with the three ordered wagons, Vichers also sent a 1931 Vickers Carden-Loyd amphibious wagon free of charge.

All four vehicles arrived in Finland in October 1933, undergoing very selective tests, also con-ducted on snow-covered terrain, which highlighted the defects and shortcomings of the various wagons. Following these tests, the Vickers Carden Loyd model 1931 amphibious tank was found to be completely unsuitable and returned after only 17 days, while both the small Vickers Carden Loyd Mk VI B tankette and the Vickers Carden-Loyd M / 1933 tank were considered suitable. for training purposes only[1].

Specifically, the Vichers Carden-Loyd M / 1922 was judged positively with regard to technical reliability and speed on the road, but negatively for mobility in snow-covered terrain and for arma-ment.

The Vickers 6-Ton wagon was instead considered suitable for the demanding conditions of use in the Finnish territory and, on 20 July 1936, the Ministry of Defense issued an order for the purchase of 32 units. For budget reasons, the tanks were purchased without weapons, optics, radios and var-ious other tools. As armament, the Swedish 37 mm Bofors cannon, built in Finland under license and named 37 Psv.K / 36, and the 7.62 mm coaxial machine gun M / 09-31 were chosen, while the German Zeiss TZF were the optics selected and order.

The delivery of the wagons by Vickers was planned in three batches:
- 11 wagons on July 20, 1937
- 10 wagons on 1 April 1938
- 11 wagons on January 1, 1939

The expected deliveries were not respected: in 1937 no wagon was delivered, in 1938 16 were de-livered, followed by another 10 in 1939 and the last 6 in 1940. In February 1939 33 guns 37 Psv.K / 36 were ordered to VTT (Valtion tykkitehdas - state gun factory), while Germany blocked the order of

---

1 The Vickers Carden-Loyd Mk IVB was used for training and survived the war, now it is exhibited in the Parola Tank Museum; the Vichers Carden-Loyd M / 1933 was also used for training until its demolition during the continuation war.

the Zeiss optics. Following the delay in the delivery of the tanks by the Vichers, the guns, the optics and the radios, no tanks were available at the outbreak of the war.

The 26 tanks that arrived by 1939 were delivered to the Panssaripataljoona and 2 were transferred in the same year to the Erillinen Panssarieskadroona (autonomous armored squadron) of the Ratsuväkiprikaati (Cavalry Brigade). In order to allow the carrying out of the fire exercises, the 37 mm Puteaux guns recovered from the FT-17s were temporarily mounted on the Vichers.

In the summer of 1937 there was also a modest upgrade of the FT-17 naaras tanks, with the replacement of the worn and unreliable 8 mm Hotchkiss M / 1914 machine guns, with new 7.62 Maxim M / 09-31 machine guns. mm air-cooled.

If news began to be felt for the armored component after long years of neglect, as far as the armored component was concerned, the situation was absolutely immobile. There was no armored car in service and no department had been set up with the aim of exploiting this vehicle. Finally, on July 27, 1936, a Panssariosasto (armored unit) was set up in Lappeenranta within the Ratsuväkiprikaati, and a new Landsverck 182 armored car purchased in Sweden was delivered. In January 1938 the ward was transformed into an Erillinen Panssarieskadroona, with the consistency of a company. The program to upgrade the armored units involved the purchase of an additional 27 Landsverck 8-ton armored cars[2], armed with a 37 mm cannon and two 7.62 mm machine guns, which would have allowed the establishment of an armored cavalry battalion. This program was never implemented, so the only armored vehicle in service in the Erillinen Panssarieskadroona remained the only Landsverk 182. During 1939 the small unit received 2 Vickers 6-Ton and 8 FT-17 tanks. The 8 FT-17s were returned after a few months with the hypothesis of replacing them with a further 5 Vickers 6-Ton, but this rotation did not happen and also the two Vichers already in service, however unarmed, were returned shortly afterwards.

▲ Parade of FT-17 tanks in Helsinki on May 16, 1920 (SA-kuva Archive).

---

2 Almost certainly it was the Landsverck L-180 armored car.

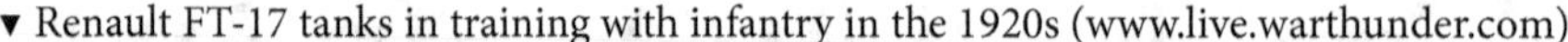

▲ Carri armati Renault FT-17 in addestramento con la fanteria negli anni'20 (www.live.warthunder.com)

▼ Renault FT-17 tanks in training with infantry in the 1920s (www.live.warthunder.com)

▲ FT-17 tank in training (SA-kuva archive).

▲ The Vickers-Carden-Loyd M / 1933 light tank tested by the Finnish army and then used for training until the Continuation War (SA-kuva Archive).

▼ A newly delivered 6-Ton Vickers tank without armament (SA-kuva Archive).

▲ A Vickers 6-Ton tank, still unarmed, during the tests (https://it.topwar.ru).

▼ Vickers 6-Ton tank photographed during the maneuvers of the summer of 1939. Note the 37 Puteaux cannon coming from an FT-17 temporarily installed to be able to carry out the maneuvers with fire, even if only with blanks. (SA-kuva archive).

▲ Five 6-Ton Vickers tanks engaged in the 1939 summer maneuvers (SA-kuva Archive).

▼ A Vickers 6-Ton tank, with its crew, at Hämeenlinna in the winter of 1940 (SA-kuva Archive).

▲ Vickers 6-Ton tanks from Pansaaripataljoona parade in Hämeenlinna just before the start of the Winter War (SA-kuva Archive).

▼ An armored 6-Ton Vickers tank, with 37mm Bofors cannon, assigned to 4th Company in December 1939 (www.waralbum.ru).

▲ Vickers 6-Ton tanks in training in the summer of 1939 (SA-kuva Archive).

"TALVISOTA" – THE WINTER WAR

After a few months of negotiations, held in Moscow and ended on November 13, 1939 with the return of the Finnish delegation to Helsinki, without reaching any solution, on November 30 the Soviet troops attacked the Finnish positions, starting the Russian war. -Finnish, better known as Talvisota, the Winter War. The Soviet attack was carried out by four armies: the 14th on the far north front with the aim of conquering the port of Petsamo and then joining the 9th to the south; the 9th with the task of cutting Finland in two by conquering the Gulf of Bothnia, thus preventing connections with Sweden; the 7th and 8th are deployed around Lake Lagoda and on the Karelian Isthmus, with the task of breaking through the Mannerheim Line, occupying Viipuri and heading towards the capital Helsinki. The Soviet Union employed over 425,000 men, about 2,500 tanks, over 2,300 aircraft and 2,000 guns. The Finns were able to oppose, to this physical and material power, about 250,000 men and women, 548 guns and 115 aircraft.

Despite this clear military supremacy, Finnish troops resisted until March 1940, when they were forced to ask for an armistice.

The war was fought during a particularly inclement winter, with temperatures even down to -70° and heavy snowfall that put the wheeled and tracked vehicles in serious difficulty, forcing them to operate along the few viable roads, which were easily interrupted.

To face the thousands of Soviet tanks, including T-26, T-37, T-38, T-28 and BT-5, and the hundreds of FAI, BA-3, BA-6, BA-10 and BA armored cars -20, the Finns could only oppose the following means:

- 34 Renault FT-17 (obsolete and partly disarmed)
- 26 Vickers 6-Ton (largely unarmed)
- 1 Landsverk 182

as well as a Vickers Carden-Loyd M / 1933 and a Vickers Carden Loyd Mk VI B usable for training purposes only.

Following the general mobilization, in October 1939, the increase in personnel allowed the Panssaripataljoona to be structured on five companies: the 1st and 2nd equipped with FT-17, the 3rd and 4th of Vickers 6-Ton while the 5th, having no wagons, it was used as a reserve of personnel to replace the losses in the other companies. Not being able to use the Vickers tanks yet, because waiting to be completed, the only tanks available in the first months of the conflict were the old Renault FT-17s.

Being well aware that sending such obsolete vehicles to the front was to be considered a suicidal action, it was decided to use them for anti-tank combat training and for the recovery of Soviet vehicles captured on the battlefield[3].

In October 1939, 11 male FT-17s and 9 female FT-17s were in service in the 1st and 2nd companies, however, it is not certain whether further tanks were, or not, received in the following months.

In February 1940, the order came to transfer the tanks of the two companies along the defensive lines and bury them as bunkers, allowing the infantry to use them as an observatory or as defensive positions, using the machine guns supplied, increasing the firepower of the infantry deployed at defense of the line of resistance.

On February 14, five FT-17s, belonging to the 1st Company, were buried at the front line near Lake Näykkijärvi, they were the only tanks that sustained firefights with the Soviets. At the Kämärä railway station the Soviets captured 8 FT-17s waiting to be unloaded from the train to be transport-

---

3 With the help of FT 17 tanks, at least 27 Soviet tanks were recovered and transferred to the Panssarikeskuskorjaamo (Armored Repair Center).

ed and buried as bunkers in the first line. Another FT-17 tank was captured by the Soviets at Pero station.

In February 10 2nd Company FT-17 tanks were transported to the Taipale Defensive Sector, where they were to be buried in the Volossula-Kaarnajoki-Linnakangas Defensive Line. Since the construction of this line was never really started, few tanks were transferred to the Takala line, a defensive line positioned on the Taipale peninsula, and buried to be used as bunker by the infantry.

In March, two unarmed FT-17 tanks were sent to the island of Vuoratsu, north of Lake Lagoda, with the task of delivering messages and evacuating the wounded, tasks that were never carried out by the two tanks.

With the tanks used as bunkers, the 1st and 2nd companies were disbanded and the personnel were transferred to the Tank Battalion headquarters in Hämeenlinna, where they were used for training recruits and in the repair shop. At the Erillinen panssarivaunujoukkue (Autonomous Tank Platoon) of the Niinisalo training center, four FT-17 tanks were present in March 1940.

At the end of the war only 4 FT-17s were still in service, they were then used for training until 1943 and then demolished[4].

The 3rd and 4th companies began training in Hämeenlinna with the unarmed Vickers 6-Ton tanks, only during the maneuvers carried out in the summer of 1939 some tanks were provisionally armed with the 37 mm Puteaux guns recovered from the FT-17s. Although the delivery by the VTT of the 37 mm guns and optics had been accelerated, the first fully assembled tank was delivered to the 4th company only on December 14, followed by 6 other tanks on January 6, 1940, by 1 tank on January 12 and finally from 10 floats on February 8.

Due to the shortage of ready-to-fight tanks, the Panssaripataljoona Command decided to assign all 6-Ton armed Vichers to the 4th Company, while the 3rd was awaiting the arrival of the completed tanks continuing the training, as well as being used as a backup personnel.

Only from the month of January the 4th company was therefore able to begin training in fire and combat by platoons, completing it, in an accelerated manner, by February, without having been able to train in joint maneuvers with the infantry.

The 4th company was under the command of Lieutenant O. Heinonen, while the three platoons were under the command of the lieutenants of the reserve: V. Mikkola the 1st, O. Voionmaa the 2nd and S. Sirmio the 3rd.

On February 23, 1940, the company, with a supply of 16 Vickers 6-Ton tanks, was declared ready for combat and immediately sent to the front, where it headed with 13 tanks, five motorcycles, two cars and twelve trucks. Almost certainly 3 chariots were left with the 3rd company to complete the training.

On 24 February the company was loaded onto a railway train that transported it from Hämeen-linna to Hovinmaa, northwest of Viipuri in the Isthmus of Karelia, at the disposal of the command of the II Board of Directors, placing the base of operations at the Markovilla Petty Officer School. of operational orders.

The new Soviet offensive in the Karelian Isthmus, carried by 18 divisions belonging to the 7th and 13th Army, had begun on 1 February, after strong bombardments by heavy artillery had compromised many of the defensive works of the Mannerhein Line. Following the battle of the Lähde road, fought from 11 to 14 February, the Soviet troops managed to break through the defensive line, forcing the Finns to retreat towards the V-line (Valilinja), a defensive line only sketched and without defensive works permanent, reached by the Soviets on 17. Continuing the offensive pressure, wards of the 123rd Division and the 35th Armored Brigade managed to create a salient in the Finnish defenses, creating a narrow corridor at the Honkaniemi station. Despite numerous counterattacks,

---

4 Only one example of the Renault FT 17 was preserved, today it is exhibited in the Parola Tank Museum.

the Finnish troops failed to clear the dangerous corridor, thus giving the Soviets the opportunity, on February 23, to start circumventing Finnish positions.

In an attempt to counter the danger of being surrounded, the II C.d.A. he planned a counterattack, which was to be carried out by units belonging to the 23rd Division, to be carried out on the morning of the 26th. The action involved the use of four Jäeger battalions, two artillery battalions and the 4th Vickers tank company. Colonel Woldemar, commander of the 23rd Division, summoned the commanders of the departments involved in the following morning's action to his command on the evening of 25 February. Captain Kunnas, commander of the 3rd Jäeger, and Lieutenant Heinonen, in command of the 4th Tank Company, departments that should have started the offensive, asked to postpone the attack for at least 24 hours, to allow an accurate reconnaissance of the terrain. , the recognition of the position of the enemy and a greater integration of the two departments, given that until then the infantry had never cooperated together with the tanks. The proposal was rejected and the attack was confirmed for 6 am on 26 February.

Of the 13 tanks available to the company, only 8 managed to reach the starting base for the attack, the other 5 were blocked along the way due to engine failures due to petrol which, not having received the addition of paraffin, it froze in the pipes. Two other tanks suffered engine failures when they had already reached the starting base for the attack, thus leaving the six remaining tanks the honor of the first fight by the Finnish tank departments.

The plan of attack provided for the start of the artillery preparation fire at 6 am and then the assault by the tanks immediately followed by the jäegers. Unfortunately, the artillery shots, due to communication errors between the departments, hit the jäegers ready to spring for the attack, causing numerous losses and causing the action to be shifted by an hour.

At 7.15 the attack of the 6 Vickers 6-Ton of the 4th company began, under the command of Lieutenant Heinonen, who sprinted forward, badly assisted by the infantry which, among other things, was blocked by enemy fire. One tank, the R-668, was blocked by an obstacle and was abandoned, the remaining five tanks fought hard against the T-26 formations of the 35th Soviet Light Armored Brigade. Four tanks, R-648; R-667; R-670 and R-655, were hit and abandoned by their crews while the R-664 was damaged but managed to return to the starting base. At 10 am the order was given to stop the attack and retreat.

For the 4th Company, the first tank battle of the war ended in defeat, five Vickers tanks were lost and one was damaged, while three destroyed Soviet tanks were claimed.

The Russian captain Arhipov, commander of the T-26 company of the 35th Light Armored Brigade that collided in Honkaniemi, in the memoir written in the postwar period, claimed that his unit had destroyed 14 Vickers tanks and had captured 3 intact, as well as not to have suffered any loss. The statement about the destroyed and captured wagons is absolutely inaccurate, given that at that date there were 16 Vickers 6-Ton in service in total and only 6 took part in the action.

The causes of the failure were identified in the absence of radios on board the tanks, which therefore prevented communications between the vehicles and with the infantry; the lack of cooperation with the infantry, which until then had never operated together with the tanks; the lack of information on the enemy to be faced, the attack was initiated simultaneously with an offensive action by the Soviets that sent dozens of tanks assisted by infantry to attack; the difficulty due to bad weather in identifying the enemy vehicles, since the difference between the Vickers 6-Ton and the T-26 was only in the different gun and in a few other details. Captain Arhipov himself wrote that only after carefully inspecting the enemy tanks did he notice that they had a blue band around the turret that distinguished them from the Soviet tanks, in addition to the difference in the cannon.

On February 27, the order was given to the surviving tanks of the 4th Company to go to the Rautlampi area, in an anti-tank function, under the control of the 68th Infantry Regiment. On 29

February, the 1st Tank Platoon sustained several attacks by Soviet T-28 tanks, belonging to the 20th Heavy Tank Brigade, at the Vääräkoski intersection, hitting numerous enemy vehicles and destroying 2.

The 2nd platoon was instead engaged to cover the retreat of the infantry following the attack unleashed in the afternoon by the Soviet infantry, supported by heavy and light tanks, from Ahola in the direction of Pero. In the fighting, the R-672 tank was lost, which had a broken track and leaned on its side forcing the crew to abandon the vehicle and continue fighting alongside the infantry, and the R-666 tank which, under fire from five T-26s and a T-28, after having destroyed 2 opposing tanks it was in turn put out of use.

On 1 March the company was placed under the command of the 4th Division, receiving the order to move to Viipuri, with the task of reserve in anti-tank function. On March 6, the R-664 tank was ordered to support a counterattack, but, blocked due to the rocky terrain, it was hit in the engine compartment by bullets fired by two enemy tanks and was damaged, forcing the crew to sabotage it and then retreat together. to the infantrymen.

Seven days later the war ended: the 4th company had lost a total of 8 wagons out of the 13 available, as well as three trucks and a motorcycle. The losses suffered amounted to 1 fallen, 10 injured (of which 6 serious) and 8 missing, to be considered fallen,

In addition to the FT-17s and the 6-Ton Vickers supplied to the Panssaripataljoona, Landsverk 182, the only armored car in service in the Suomen Maavoimat at that time, also took part in the Winter War.

On 6 October 1939 the armored car was sent to Karelia and two days later a new unit was formed, the Moottoroitu Osasto (motorized unit), within the Ratsuväkiprikaati. The small department was equipped with an armored car, two trucks and a motorcycle. At the beginning of the war, Landsverk was deployed in Uusikirkko, in the Isthmus of Karelia and on 3 December took part in the fighting in the village of Perkjärvi, where it was used to evacuate some wounded from the front. On December 26, the unit was transferred to the front line in Taipale. On January 5, 1940 the Moottoroitu Osasto, having acknowledged that for a single vehicle it was not necessary to have a department of similar size, was suppressed,

From that date the Landsverk was used as a reserve by the Cavalry Brigade until the end of the conflict, no longer being used in combat.

On March 12, 1940, the peace treaty that put an end to hostilities was signed in Moscow, the cease-fire began at 11 am the following day. Finland, in addition to ceding the entire Karelian isthmus, with the important city of Viipuri, and a substantial portion of territory north of Lake Ladoga to the Soviet Union, also had to cede some islets in the Gulf of Finland, a part of the Rybachi peninsula, an area in the area of Salla and Kuusamo, in addition to renting the Hanko promontory for 30 years and completing the railway from Kemijärvi to the new border line in Salla, to allow the connection with the existing railway in Soviet territory . The Petsamo area, with its port, despite being occupied by the Soviets, remained instead to Finland.

▲ Soviet tank BT-5, probably belonging to the 34th Light Tank Brigade, destroyed in Lemetti on 1 February 1940 (SA-kuva Archive).

▲ Marshal Carl Gustaf Emil Mannerheim, Supreme Commander of the Finnish Armed Forces (http://heninen.net).

▲ FT-17 tank captured by the Soviets in Karelia (www.waralbum.ru).

▲ Weapons, vehicles and a BT-7 tank abandoned by the Soviets in the Finnish forest (www.waralbum.ru).

▼ Column of Soviet T-20 "Komsomolets" 1st series light tractors, with 45 mm anti-tank guns in tow, of the 44th Infantry Division, destroyed and abandoned on the road to Suomussalmi in January 1940 (www.waralbum.ru).

▲ An abandoned Soviet T-20 "Komsomolets" light tractor inspected by Finnish soldiers (www.waralbum.ru).

▼ Soviet armored car BA-20 captured by the Finns (www.waralbum.ru).

▲ Soviet armored car BA-20 put out of the US on March 20, 1940 in Oinassalmi and captured by the Finns (SA-kuva Archive).

▼ Soviet light amphibious tank T-37 abandoned and captured by the Finns in December 1939 on the road in the Tolvajärvi area (www.waralbum.ru).

▲ Vickers 6-Ton armored tank of the 4th Company knocked out by the Soviets during the battle of Honkaniemi on February 23, 1940 (https://it.topwar.ru).

▼ The Vickers 6-Ton R-666 and R-672 tanks destroyed during the rearguard action to counter the Soviet advance towards the town of Pero on February 29, 1940 (SA-kuva Archive).

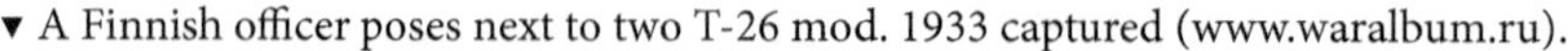

▲ A tank OT-26 mod. 1931 Soviet abandoned in March 1940 (SA-kuva Archive).

▼ A Finnish officer poses next to two T-26 mod. 1933 captured (www.waralbum.ru).

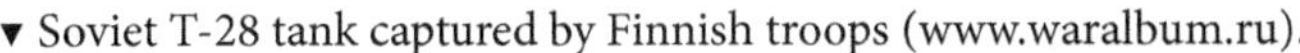

▲ Tank T-26 mod. 1937 belonging to the 40th Light Tank Brigade captured by the Finns (www.suomensotilas.fi).

▼ Soviet T-28 tank captured by Finnish troops (www.waralbum.ru).

▲ One of the two Soviet T-28 tanks captured intact while being transferred to the rear (www.waralbum.ru).

▼ The prototype of the SMK heavy tank, in service in a company of the 91st Tank Battalion of the 20th Heavy Tank Brigade, jumped on a mine and abandoned in the field in the Summa sector in January 1940. It was recovered by the Soviets only after the armistice (www .waralbum.ru).

FROM PEACE TO CONTINUATION WAR

The Soviet Union had emerged victorious from the conflict, but the victory had paid a high price, with tens of thousands killed, wounded and missing, as well as the loss of thousands of vehicles of all kinds.

The Finns captured hundreds of armored and armored vehicles on their territory, which they repaired to be put back into service in their army. As the small Panssaripataljoona workshop in Hämeenlinna was unable to repair and / or overhaul the large number of captured Soviet tanks, on 15 December 1939 it was decided to build the Panssarikeskuskorjaamo, a centralized repair shop for armored vehicles in Varkaus, at some buildings of the Alström JSC factory. Under the command of Major Ruotsi, non-commissioned officers and enlisted men, along with civilian mechanics and foreign volunteers[5], they managed in a short time to install equipment and machine tools, allowing the workshop to start repairs on the dozens of vehicles that were transported from the battlefields[6].

Almost intact vehicles, slightly damaged vehicles and other unrecoverable vehicles were brought to Varkaus because they were destroyed and / or burned, together with disassembled parts to the tanks that had not been possible to transport, including the turrets complete with cannons and machine guns, using the materials recovered as pieces replacement. Every vehicle that arrived was registered and numbered. During the Winter War, over 300 vehicles of all types arrived in Varkaus.

At least 131 tanks were recovered between T-26 mod. 1931, T-26 mod. 1933, T-26 mod. 1938[7], OT-26, OT-130[8], T-28, BT-5, T-37, T-38; 21 armored cars, D-8, FAI, BA-6, BA-10, BA-20, and 62 light tractors T-20 Komsomolets[9] arrived at the Panssarikeskuskorjaamo to be restored and reused.

In January 1941 the total of T-26 tanks, repaired and ready to be sent to the departments, was 47, of which 5 T-26A and 42 between T-26B and T-26C. The few actions that had involved the Vickers 6-Ton had shown the low effectiveness of the 37 mm gun against Soviet tanks, especially against the T-28 medium tank. Given the large availability of 45 mm guns, including ammunition, the remaining 26 6-Ton Vickers were rearmed with the 45 mm 20K mod. 1934 and the 7.62 mm Degtjarëv DT coaxial machine gun, being called T-26E (Englantilainen - British).

In addition to recovering and restoring the huge spoils of war captured by the Soviets during the Winter War, the Finnish Commands carefully studied the causes that had led to the defeat of Honkaniemi and the loss of so many tanks during the clashes with the enemy. Thus, new tactics for the use of tanks were developed, cooperation with the infantry improved, training improved, the installation of radios on vehicles completed and the armored battalion restructured.

With the arrival of new vehicles, the Panssaripataljoona was structured around:
- 1st - 2nd - 3rd Armored Company - each with 15/16 tanks between T-26B / T-26C / T-26E plus 3 T-26A

5 On February 21, 1940, an Italian officer, a Belgian officer and a Belgian soldier arrived in Varkaus and lent their work in restoring the vehicles captured and brought in for repair. A Swedish company donated to Panssarikeskuskorjaamo machine tools on which numerous Swedish mechanics worked, from November 1941 to December 1942 there were about sixty, carrying out the most complex tasks, contributing with their work to the repair of dozens of vehicles.

6 In addition to the Varkaus workshop, civil plants were also involved in the restoration of the captured vehicles: Lokomo AO, Rosenlev, Ruona AO and Ahlström, in addition to the military workshop in Hameenlinna.

7 The Finns used the following designation for captured T-26 tanks: T-26 Model 1931 (equipped with two turrets with machine guns) T-26A; T-26 Model 1933 (with riveted turret) T-26B; T-26 Model 1937 (with welded turret) T-26C.

8 Tanks OT-26 and OT-130 were the flamethrower version of the T-26 model 1931, where instead of the machine gun in a turret, and T-26 model 1933, where instead of the 45 mm gun a flamethrower was installed. During the Winter War the Finns captured 2 OT-26 and 4 OT-130 from the Soviets, while in the Continuation War 4 OT-133 were captured.

9 In total, the T-20 Komsomolets light tractors captured by the Finns during the Winter and Continuation Wars amount to over 210, of which 202 were assigned to the departments.

- a heavy tank platoon equipped with 2 T-28 and 2 T-26 tanks
- a flamethrower tank platoon with 4 OT-130s
- two reconnaissance platoons with 5 T-37 or T-38 amphibious tanks

Commander of the armored battalion, Lieutenant Colonel Bjorkman was appointed.

Thanks to the work of the workshops for the restoration of the captured vehicles, as of May 31, 1941 the tanks in service in the Finnish units were the following:

- 29 T-37A
- 13 between T-38 and T-38M
- 10 T-26A
- 20 T-26B
- 4 T-26C
- 26 T-26E
- 2 OCT-26
- 4 OT-130
- 2 T-28

None of the 22 armored cars, captured and repaired, was assigned to the Panssaripataljoona, instead they were all assigned to armored platoons serving in infantry divisions as reconnaissance units.

▲ Soviet tanks, captured during the Winter War, at the Varkaus depot in the spring of 1940, waiting to be reused (www.hameensanomat.fi).

▲ Captured OT-130 flamethrower tank photographed during repairs at the Panssarikeskuskorjaamo, the main armored vehicle repair facility, in April 1940. Two 6-Ton Vickers with nationality insignia, white-blue, can be seen on the right. -white, painted around the turret, in use during the winter war. (SA-kuva archive).

▼ Soviet OT-130 flamethrower tank, abandoned by the Soviets during the Winter War, being recovered by the Finnish units (SA-kuva Archive).

▲ One of the two T-28 tanks captured during the winter war, during tests in Varkaus in April 1940 (SA-kuva Archive)

▼ A T-28 tank captured from the Soviets, reconditioned in the Varkaus workshop and delivered to the Finnish army (SA-kuva archive).

▲ Recovery of captured T-26 tanks near the village of Ruhtinaanmäki, in the foreground a T-26 mod. 1937, in the background a T-26 mod. 1931 with two turrets (www.waralbum.ru).

▲ A Soviet T-20 "Komsomolets" light tractor reused by the Finns after repair (www.palasuomenhistoriaa.net).

▼ A T-38 amphibious tank, captured by the Soviets, overhauled and delivered to the Finnish army (www.waralbum.ru).

"JATKOSOTA" – THE CONTINUATION WAR

The application of the harsh clauses provided by the peace treaty, the economic crisis, the presence of tens of thousands of refugees who fled the territories ceded to the Soviet Union, the belief, on the part of the political and military leaders, that the Soviets would soon return the attack to conquer Finland, in addition to the constant pressure exerted by the Soviet Union, quickly pushed the country into the German orbit. Germany, which as early as August 1940 had requested permission for the passage of its troops to Norway in exchange for the sale of arms, obtaining the consent of the Finnish, drew up the plans for the operations, to be carried out in close cooperation between the German and Finnish troops, as part of the more complex "Barbarossa" operation.

In May 1941, the German plans were presented to the Finnish military leaders, who tacitly accepted them in subsequent meetings held in Helsinki in early June. On June 16, 1941, general mobilization was proclaimed. The "Barbarossa" operation began on 22 June. On June 25, 1941, the Finnish troops began the offensive against the Soviet troops deployed on the armistice line of March 1940, it was the beginning of the so-called Continuation War, alongside the German ally.

In July the Panssaripataljoona was merged with the 1st Jääkäri / Jäeger Brigade, forming a reinforced Jäeger Brigade under the command of Colonel Ernst Ruben Lagus. Between 12 and 18 August 1941, some BT-5 and BT-7 tanks captured intact from the Soviets, were assigned to the heavy tank platoon, which ceded its 2 T-26s to the 1st and 3rd tank companies[10], constituting the Christie-Osasto (Christie Detachment), consisting of 3 BT-5 and 2 BT-7 wagons. With the arrival of the new vehicles, the heavy tank platoon was made up as follows:

- 2 T-28 tanks
- 3 BT-5 tanks
- 2 BT-7 tanks
- 4 trucks (maintenance, ammunition, fuel and supplies)
- 1 car

The BT tanks were used as support for the infantry, for which a detached Jäeger infantry unit was created, called Kevyt Osasto 4 (Light Detachment 4), trained to fight like the Soviet infantry transported on tanks, and inserted into the heavy tank platoon . Each BT had a squad consisting of a non-commissioned officer and six infantrymen who were carried on the back of the wagon and dismounted when they had to fight.

The 1st Jääkäri / Jäeger Brigade, in the first months of the war, was not particularly involved in the fighting, the armored battalion remained available behind the front line until early September. On 3 September, the Finnish offensive took place on the front of Lake Lagoda. On the 6th the troops under the command of Colonel Lagus, departed from Tuulosjoki, conquered Olonctz, on the 7th they reached the Svir' river[11], between Lake Lagoda and Lake Onega, and on the 8th they interrupted the railway line that leads from Murmansk to Lodejnoe Pole. The chariots of the Panssaripataljoona participated in the battle of Tuulos and subsequently contributed to the conquest of the city of Petrozavodsk[12], fell into Finnish hands on 1 October.

The heavy tank platoon was used in the initial fighting on September 4, which had both T-28s hit and damaged by Soviet anti-tank shots, while the Christie-Osasto showed all the difficulty of the

---

10 A total of 62 BT-5 and 53 BT-7 tanks were captured during the Continuation War.
11 Svir' river for the Finns it was named Syväri.
12 The city of Petrozavodsk, for the Finns Petroskoi, after its conquest was renamed Äänislinna during the Continuation War.

BT tanks to move on muddy ground. In fact, 2 BT-5s got stuck in the mud unable to participate in the action. On day 5, 2 BT tanks were sent in pursuit of the retreating Soviet troops, but were hit by the anti-tanks that destroyed the BT-7 R-100. On the 7th the platoon, with the remaining chariots, continued the advance from Aunus to the river Svir'. Between 13 and 14 September all the four remaining BT wagons were out of order due to mechanical breakdowns or breakdowns. Since it was not possible to carry out the repair on site, the vehicles were sent to Varkaus on the 16th and the Christie-Osasto was dissolved on the 17th. Thus ended the brief war experience of the BT tanks in the Panssaripataljoona.

Leaving a company on Svir', the armored battalion was transferred to the northern front of Lake Onega, where from 9 November it took part in the offensive that led to the conquest of Medvežegorsk and Povenetz on 4 and 5 December. The company remaining on Svir' participated in the fighting near the villages of Lobskaya and Gora on the eastern bank of the river. In mid-December 1941 the offensive ended and the Finnish troops entrenched themselves on the line reached, which remained unchanged until the resumption of the conflict in June 1944.

The Panssaripataljoona was transferred to the reserve in the Petrozavodsk area.

The victorious offensive in Karelia, in addition to allowing the Finns to cross the old border line of 1939 and to conquer vast areas of Soviet Karelia, allowed the Soviets to capture dozens and dozens of armored vehicles. In addition to several medium and heavy tanks, including T-28, KV-1 and T-34, there were still many amphibious and T-26 tanks, along with some OT-133 flamethrower tanks, captured intact or damaged. Furthermore, unlike the Winter War where most of the BT tanks had been abandoned on the ground because they were unable to recover them due to the lack of suitable means, in addition to the fact that many were burned, during this phase there were dozens of BT-5 tanks. and BT-7 captured intact or slightly damaged. As seen above, however, the Finns did not consider the wagon valid and were not introduced into service except in very few specimens.

Dozens of turrets were then identified from the BT tanks and used to arm the forts and bunkers of the defensive lines, while a few hulls were used for the construction of the assault guns. Thanks to the availability of new tanks, at the beginning of 1942 a second armored battalion was formed on two tank companies. In February 1942 the heavy tank platoon was transformed into the Raskas Panssarikomppania heavy tank company, equipped with 1 T-34 and 6 T-28.

After a few months, the available tanks had become: 3 T-34, 2 KV-1, 7 T-28 and 1 T-50.

February 10, 1942[13] the order of service was issued concerning the constitution of the Panssariprikaati Armored Brigade, officially constituted on March 9, which was to be composed of three tank battalions, of which the third equipped with medium tanks T-28, T-34 and BT-5 / 7. Since the number of medium tanks captured at the time was not sufficient, the plan was modified by inserting a Panssaritykkipataljoona (Assault Gun Battalion) in place of the third tank battalion. In June 1942, the Päämaja (Armed Forces Headquarters) issued the order to form this battalion called Rynnäkkötykkipataljoona (Assault Gun Battalion).

The Panssariprikaati was made up of:
* two armored battalions
* an assault gun battalion
* a self-propelled anti-aircraft battery since May

In April, some units of the Brigade participated in the counter-offensive in Karelia, in the Rapovanmaki area, to repel a Soviet attack, losing 4 T-26 tanks.

Between May and June a new reorganization of the two armored battalions was carried out:
* 1st Battalion - 1st and 2nd Company: each with 17 T-26, 3rd Company: 3 T-34, 3 T.28, 5 T-26
* 2nd Battalion - 4th and 5th Company: each with 17 T-26, 6th Company: 2 KV-1, 4 T-28, 5 T-26

---

13 According to other sources, the order to establish the Panssariprikaati was issued on 23 February.

THE PANSSARIDIVISIOONA

On 28 June 1942 the General Staff decided to set up the Panssaridivisioona, aggregating the Armored Brigade to the Jäeger Brigade. The Division, de facto established on 30 June, was constituted as follows:

- Divisional Headquarters
- Jäeger Brigade
- 2nd Jäeger Battalion
- 3rd Jäeger Battalion
- 4th Jäeger Battalion
- Motorcyclists company
- Armored Brigade Panssariprikaati
- 1st Armored Battalion
- 2nd Armored Battalion
- Assault gun battalion
- Artillery Regiment
- 14th Heavy Cannon Battalion
- Two light gun battalions
- Counter-tank artillery battalion
- Engineer battalion
- Self-propelled anti-aircraft artillery battery
- Armored transmission company
- Various services

The wagons in service in the Panssaridivisioona, divided between the two Panssaripataljoona, were the following:

- 80 T-26 (between B / C / E)
- 7 T-28
- 3 T-34
- 2 KV-1
- 6 self-propelled anti-aircraft Landsverk L-62 Anti II[14] in the anti-aircraft battery
- 4 between T-37 and T-38 in the transmissions company

In the counter-tank battalion the PaK 38 guns were towed by the T-20 Komsomolets light tractors. The command of the Panssaridivisioona was assigned to Major General Ernst Ruben Lagus.

The means to arm the Assault Cannon Battalion were not present in the arsenal of the Finnish army, so the VTT was ordered to design a new vehicle based on the BT-7 tank armed with the British Ordnance QF 4.5in howitzer . 114 mm MK 2 called 114 H / 18. VTT, in collaboration for some work with Oy Lokomo Ab and Crichton-Vulcan, built by early September 1942 a BT-7 tank equipped with a very high and wide turret containing the 114 H / 18 howitzer and sent it to Field Test Battalion. The tank was officially named 15 tonnin rynnäkkötykkipansarivaunu BT-42 (15-ton BT-42 assault tank), commonly called BT-42. 18 BT-42s were ordered to arm three companies of 6 vehicles each. The tests to which the BT-42 was subjected gave a poor result, the vehicle was deemed unsatisfactory and numerous modifications were required. The first modified BT-42s were delivered

---

14 The Luftvärnskanonvagn L-62 anti II, better known as Landsverk L-62 Anti II, was a self-propelled anti-aircraft aircraft designed and built in Sweden at Finnish request. In Finland the vehicle was designated ItPsv 41, Ilmatorjuntapanssarivaunu 41 (Anti-aircraft tank 41). It was armed with a 40mm Bofors L / 60 anti-aircraft gun.

to the 1st company on February 26, 1943, followed in March by the vehicles for the 2nd and in May for those of the 3rd. The delivery of all 18 BT-42s, several months later than expected, took place by the end of 1943. In addition to repairing and overhauling damaged and / or recovered tanks on the battlefields, and building the new BT-42 assault guns, the Varkaus workshop also replaced the engine of all the BA-6 and BA armored cars. -10 captured from the Soviets and assigned to various Finnish units. The 50hp GAZ-AA and GAZ-MM engines were replaced with the more powerful 95hp Ford V-8 engines, allowing the armored cars a marked improvement in performance on difficult Finnish terrain. The division spent the remaining months of 1942 completing training, remaining in operational reserve at the rear of the front. In the spring of 1943 it was transferred to the Aunus front, where it operated as a tactical reserve.

In March 1943 the command of the Panssaridivisioona proposed to convert 20 BT-7 tanks into troop transport. At first rejected, after a few months the proposal to convert 14 BT-7 into armored troop transport vehicles was accepted. Work on the prototype began in Varkaus on 18 May, work which was completed by October with the transfer of the vehicle to the 3rd Jäeger Battalion on 11 November for field tests. The new vehicle, called BT-43 and registered Ps. 611-1, it could carry 10 soldiers, but was not further modified after the requests made after the tests. Equipped with a wooden box, coming from a truck, it was later used as an ammunition carrier.

In the months of June and July 1943, the 1st company of the assault battalion was sent to the front area on the Svir River, to assess the operation of the BT-42 in the field. The 1st company consisted of the BT-42 R-704, R-708, R-710, R-713 and R-717. Used to destroy bunkers and defensive positions equipped with machine guns, with direct and indirect fire actions, they proved their effectiveness by annihilating and damaging hundreds of enemy positions, but at the same time also having no anti-tank and off-road capability. During this operational cycle, due to enemy fire, the 1st company suffered the loss of one dead and one wounded, as well as having the BT-42 R-710 slightly damaged.

Despite having demonstrated its usefulness as a self-propelled gun, the BT-42 was deemed unsuitable for the originally intended role of assault gun, such as that played by the Stugs in German armored divisions.

In May 1943, having acknowledged the deficiencies of the BT-42 as an assault gun, the Päämaja requested the German ally to supply 45 Sturmgeschütz III Ausf assault guns. G. The Germans declared their willingness to sell a total of 30 Stug III Ausf. G within the year[15], as well as providing training staff.

The Stug III Ausf G, transported by ship, were delivered by the Germans in three batches:
- July 6, 1943: 10
- August 10, 1943: 8
- September 3, 1943: 12

All the vehicles, new and painted in dunkelgelb, were transferred to the Panssarikeskus where they were repainted with the standard Finnish three-tone camouflage, received the nationality markings and the Ps numbering, replaced the MG-34 with the Soviet DT machine gun installed on the folding shield on the roof of the casemate. On 2 September the Stu 40Gs began to be delivered to the Rynnäkkötykkipataljoona, which was able to sell the BT-42s.

At the battalion all the Stu 40Gs were subjected to other changes regarding:
- Removal of schürtzen and attachment points
- Addition of a wooden crate to the rear above the engine compartment to hold various tools
- Reposition of the spare wheels on the sides of the hull on new supports.

---

15 In total there were 59 Sturmgeschütz III Ausf. G delivered to the Finns, 30 in 1943 and 29 in 1944. In the Suomen Maavoimat they were inventoried as 24 tonnin rynnäkkötykki-panssarivaunu Sturmgeschütz 40, abbreviated as 24 Ryn. tyk.psv./Stu.40 or Stu 40G, but the crews simply called them "Sturmi".

The organization of the assault gun battalion was as follows:
- Command company
- Command platoon: 2 Stu 40G, 1 BA-20, 2 trucks, 3 motorcycles
- Supply Platoon: 10 trucks and 1 ambulance
- Radio platoon: Steyr Sd.Kfz vehicle. 15
- 1st Assault Gun Company
- Command platoon: 2 Stu 40G, 1 BA-20, 1 truck
- 1st Platoon: 3 Stu 40G
- 2nd Platoon: 3 Stu 40G
- 3rd Platoon: without means until August 1944
- Maintenance team: 1 Kubelwaben, 1 truck
- Refueling Platoon: 3 Ford Maultiers, 4 trucks, 1 ambulance
- 2nd Assault Gun Company
- Command platoon: 2 Stu 40G, 1 BA-20, 1 truck
- 1st Platoon: 3 Stu 40G
- 2nd Platoon: 3 Stu 40G
- 3rd Platoon: without means until August 1944
- Maintenance team: 1 Kubelwaben, 1 truck
- Refueling Platoon: 3 Ford Maultiers, 4 trucks, 1 ambulance
- 3rd Assault Gun Company
- Command platoon: 2 Stu 40G, 1 BA-20, 1 truck
- 1st Platoon: 3 Stu 40G
- 2nd Platoon: 3 Stu 40G
- 3rd Platoon: without means until August 1944
- Maintenance team: 1 Kubelwaben, 1 truck
- Refueling Platoon: 3 Ford Maultiers, 4 trucks, 1 ambulance

Subordinated to the Rynnäkkötykkipataljoona there was also the III Platoon mobile workshops, equipped with Büssing NAG 4500 workshop trucks, Sd.Kfz half-tracks. 9 FAMO, Büssing-NAG 4500 mobile crane and other trucks.

Having solved the armament problem of the assault gun battalion, the decision on how to use the 18 BT-42s in service remained to be taken. Two options were put forward:
- Separate self-propelled artillery battery (Erillinen Panssaripatteri): equipped with 6 BT-42 used for indirect fire
- Separate tank company (Erillinen Panssarikomppania): equipped with 12 BT-42s used for direct fire

The option of the separate tank company was chosen, established in November 1943, which on 7 December received 12 BT-42s from the Rynnäkkötykkipataljoona.

Meanwhile, the intense training of the various departments continued and reached a high level of preparation so as to make the Division deserve the nickname of "Marskin Nyrkki" ("Marshal's Fist"), in reference to Marshal Mannerhein. The Panssaridivisioona was also referred to as "Laguksen Nuolet" ("Arrows of Lagus") by the divisional emblem representing three yellow and black arrows designed by Major General Lagus[16].

On February 13, 1944, the Panssaridivisioona, after spending over a year on the Aunus front,

____

16 The emblem of the Panssaridivisioona designed by Major General Lagus is still the arm badge of the soldiers of the current Armored Brigade of the Finnish Army.

was transferred to the Viipuri area, where numerous signals indicated the approach of the Soviet offensive.

As of March 17, 1944 the following vehicles were in service in the Panssaridivisioona:
* 98 T-26 between B / C / E7 T-28
* 7 T-34
* 2 KV-1
* 14 BT-42
* 4 T-38
* 1 T-50
* 6 Landsverk Anti AA
* 26 Stu 40G[17]
* 18 T-20 Komsomolets
* 20 armored cars

In June 1944 the Panssaridivisioona was structured as follows:
* Armored Division Headquarters
* Armored Brigade - Panssariprikaati
* 1st Armored Battalion (T-26 B / C / E), heavy company (T-34, T-50)
* 2nd Armored Battalion (T-26 B / C / E), heavy company (KV-1, T-28, T-34)
* Armored AA battery (Landsverk Anti II)
* Assault Cannon Battalion (Stu 40G)
* Armored Training Battalion (T-26A)
* Jäeger Brigade
* 2nd Jäeger Battalion
* 3rd Jäeger Battalion
* 4th Jäeger Battalion
* 5th Jäeger Battalion
* Jäeger anti-tank battalion (Pak 38 and Pak 40 towed by T-20 Komsomolets light tractors)
* 14th Heavy Artillery Battalion
* 6th Signal Battalion
* 2nd Pioneer Battalion
* Erillinen Panssarikomppania (BT-42)

The staff was 9,345 men on duty.

The Soviet intelligence evaluated the vehicles in service in the Panssaridivisioona in 108 tanks, between light / medium and heavy, and 24 assault guns, very close to the real consistency of the vehicles in service in the division, demonstrating a high capacity of investigation on the field.

On 4 June 1944, on the occasion of the seventy-seventh birthday of Marshal Mannerheim, a military parade was held in Enso, in the presence of the Finnish President Ryti, with the participation of dozens of tanks and assault guns, including T-26, T- 28, T-34/76, BT-42, Stu 40G, BA-20, T-20 tractors with Pak in tow.

By June 10, the organization of Erillinen Panssarikomppania was changed to the following structure:
* Command Platoon: 2 BT-42s
* 1st Platoon: 3 BT-42

---

17 According to other sources, 23 Stu 40Gs were in service.

- 2ⁿᵈ Platoon: 3 BT-42
- 3ʳᵈ Platoon: 3 BT-42

For a total of 11 BT-42s instead of the 14 in service in the previous organization, which included 2 vehicles in the command platoon and 6 vehicles for each of the 2 platoons. There were 5 officers, 17 non-commissioned officers and 65 soldiers.

In the period between June and August, the Germans delivered another 29 Stu 40Gs in 5 batches:

- June 29, 1944: 5
- July 2, 1944: 7
- July 6, 1944: 3
- August 3, 1944: 6
- August 6, 1944: 8

The two years of trench warfare had allowed the Soviet Union to train new troops and strengthen considerably. After liberating Leningrad from the siege in January 1944, the Stavka decided that the time had come to destroy the Finnish army, force Finland to ask for peace and restore the borders to what was established in 1940. To achieve these objectives, plans were drawn up. offensives on two fronts: the first from Leningrad towards Viborg to the Kymi River in the Karelian Isthmus, the second from the Svir River to the 1940 border in Soviet Karelia. To face these offensives, the Soviets employed 3 Armies on the Leningrad front and 2 on the Karelia front, for a total of over 450,000 men, 800 tanks, 10,500 guns and 1,600 aircraft. To face this mass of men and vehicles, Finland could initially oppose only 75,000 men, which subsequently rose to 268,000, 1,930 guns, 110 tanks (of which only 30/40 modern) and 248 aircraft (only 50 modern). The odds ratio was 1.7: 1 for men, 5.2: 1 in guns, 6/7: 1 in planes and tanks. However, considering only the modern vehicles in service in the Finnish army, the ratio was 20: 1 for tanks and planes.

The Finnish army had set up three defensive lines in the Karelian isthmus, the main line, built along the front line reached in 1941, the VT line (Vammelsuu-Taipale) 20 km behind the main line and the VKT line (Viipuri- Kuparsaari-Taipale), While the first two had been reinforced even if not completed, the VKT line was only sketchy and construction began only in May 1944. Then there was the Salpa Line, built behind the 1940 border in front of the Kymi River .

In Soviet Karelia, along the bank of the Svir River, deep defense zones were set up with concrete bunkers, trenches and obstacles.

The first offensive towards Viborg began on 10 June 1944, after a day of preparation with continuous air raids and heavy cannon fire. The defenses were already overwhelmed on the first day of fighting.

The Panssaridivisioona was immediately engaged to stem the Soviet offensive, with the Jäeger Brigade which counterattacked the 11ᵗʰ in the Pulviselkä area, but was forced to retreat due to the overwhelming superiority of the enemy. He carried out a new counterattack on June 14, in collaboration with the Rynnäkkötykkipataljoona, but the overwhelming Soviet material and numerical supremacy caused the breakthrough of the defensive line at Kuuterselkä, forcing the Jäeger to retreat with heavy losses.

The fighting in Kuuterselkä was the first to see the Rynnäkkötykkipataljoona involved. Despite the Soviet numerical superiority, the Stu 40G obtained excellent results, destroying 18 tanks and 3 enemy assault guns, with the loss of 5 vehicles: the 531-29 destroyed by a T-34/85, the 531-17 hit several times, immobilized and damaged, finally sabotaged by its crew, the 531-24 was blocked and abandoned by the crew after running out of ammunition, the 531-23 abandoned on the battlefield by the crew without knowing the cause, the 531 -1 hit and destroyed with crew losses.

On June 15, Erillinen Panssarikomppania was ordered to go to Perkjärvi, moving the 3rd platoon over a hill in the evening with some T-26E tanks and a KV-1. On the afternoon of the 17th, the commander of the company, Lieutenant Sippel, received the order to move to the eastern shore of Lake Muolaanjärvi. Two BT-42s, the 511-19 and the failed R-705 were abandoned and sabotaged south of Kivennapa and in Perkjärvi. On the evening of the 18th, after yet another transfer, the company arrived in Viipuri, where the broken BT-42 511-15 was sabotaged. On the morning of the 19th he took up his position on the hill of Kolikkoi. Although Lieutenant Sippel had suggested deploying the BT-42s as indirect fire support, the infantry commander decided instead to split the tanks in support of the infantry to provide direct fire aid against and Soviet tanks, a role not suitable for the BTs. -42 as already experienced the previous year.

On the morning of June 20, the BT-42s were all positioned at the positions set by the Viipuri defense command. In the morning the Soviet attack was launched, supported by T-34/85 tanks and ISU-122 self-propelled vehicles. Erillinen Panssarikomppania tried to counter the enemy means, but Soviet material supremacy was too clear to prevent the enemy from overwhelming the defenses.

Between 20 and 22 June the BT-42s were lost: R-712 and R-713, at the Viipuri station, sabotaged by the crews because they were blocked; the R-717 of the Sippel estate destroyed by a T-34/85 in Viipuri; 511-7 sabotaged after being stuck in a ditch in the suburb of Karjala in Viipuri; the R-702 sabotaged by the crew east of Viipuri. It should be noted that, apart from the BT-42 R-717, all the other 7 assault guns lost were due to technical failures. From 23 to 28 June the company remained in the Viipuri area and then moved south of Myllylä on 1 July.

From 25 June the entire Brigade was involved in the battle of Tali-Ihantala, effectively contributing to the defense of the Finnish defensive line. The assault cannon battalion once again stood out, destroying 39 Soviet tanks and 4 Soviet assault guns, losing the Stu 40G 531-2 and 531-3 hit several times and immobilized. Due to the heavy losses suffered, the Brigade was withdrawn from the front on June 29 for a period of rest and reorganization.

While the battle of Tali-Ihantala was still raging, on 4 July the Soviets unleashed another offensive in the Vuosalmi sector, where the Panssaridivisioona, immediately recalled to service, was sent to try to close the holes that had opened in the defensive line. The fighting lasted until July 17, when the front stabilized. From 11 to 13 July, following the loss of the Stu 40G 531-5 hit by a T-34, the assault gun battalion destroyed 14 Soviet tanks and 6 assault guns.

The harsh fighting that took place in the months of June and July 1944 had caused heavy losses of men and vehicles to the Panssaridivisioona. The Tank Brigade lost 25 T-26s between B / C / E, 8 Stu 40Gs and a third of the anti-tank battalion's T-20 tractors, while Erillinen Panssarikomppania lost 8 of its BT-42s. To replace the lost vehicles, some tanks captured by the Soviets in the last clashes were added to the staff: 7 T-34/85 and 1 ISU-152.

The fighting had shown that only the few modern medium tanks and assault guns: T-34 and Stu 40G, were now able to compete on an equal footing with Soviet vehicles, but the big difference was in the numbers. Faced with the hundreds of tanks and assault guns, more and more powerful, placed on the battlefield by the Soviets, the Finns could only oppose forty vehicles capable of being able to stand up to the adversary.

Taking note of the obsolescence of the available tanks, the headquarters of the Finnish armed forces, on 7 July 1944, decided to withdraw the T-26 A / B / C / E and the T-28 from active service, approving a plan to reorganize the two tank battalions with the introduction of new vehicles. Colonel Björkman, commander of the Brigade, again on 7 July issued the order to dissolve the Erillinen Panssarikomppania, all the surviving BT-42s had to be concentrated in Enso and then transferred to the military technical depot. On July 16, once the paperwork at the warehouse was completed, the company's history was definitively closed[18].

The reorganization of the Armored Brigade provided for the restructuring of the two Panssaripataljoona by inserting the new vehicles in delivery:

- 1st Battalion: 1st company equipped with T-34 and KV-1 tanks, 2nd and 3rd with PzKw IVJ, for a total of 30 German tanks. If all the 30 PzKw IVJs had not been available, the staff would have been integrated with Stu 40G.
- 2nd Battalion: 3 companies equipped with 40 PzKw IVJs. If the PzKw IVJs had not been delivered, the possibility of rearming the battalion with T-34 tanks sold by the Germans was foreseen.

The first battalion identified to carry out the reorganization was the 2nd, which was then transferred to the city of Lappeenranta, to begin training on the new tanks.

In the 1st Battalion in the 3rd company all 7 available T.34 / 76 were centralized, while in the 2nd were inserted the 7 T.34 / 85 tanks recovered from 25 June to 4 July in Portinhoikka and Vakkila[19], in the 1st the T-26s remained in service.

Germany agreed to supply, in the period July-October, 10 PzKw IVJ and 15 Stu 40G per month, for a total of no more than 40 PzKw IVJ. Between 26 August and 1 September 1944, the Germans delivered 15 PzKw IVJs.

However, this was the only delivery made to Finland, since, having heard of the negotiations for the stipulation of an armistice with the Soviet Union, the Germans blocked the further dispatch of PzKw IVJ and Stu 40G which on 2 September had already been loaded on the ships together with 9 T-34/76 tanks.

The 15 PzKw IVJs were delivered to the 2nd tank battalion together with some Stu 40Gs, thus allowing the formation of two mixed tank / assault gun companies and the continuation of training.

On the morning of September 4, 1944, the Finnish ceasefire came into force, following the agreements for the stipulation of the armistice which was officially signed on the 19th of the same year in Moscow. This second phase of the conflict against the Soviet Union ended with a heavy defeat, but for Finland the war was not yet over, this time the fighting would take place against the former German ally.

In the battles fought during the final Soviet offensive from June to August 1944, the units of the Finnish army lost a total of 42 tanks and assault guns and 62 light tractors, against a number of about 700 enemy vehicles. declared destroyed. In reality, the total losses suffered by the Soviet formations amounted to 294 armored vehicles.

---

18 The ten remaining BT-42 assault guns were stored at the military technical depot (Sotatekninen Varikko), but were scrapped only in 1951, minus one example now on display at the Parola Tank Museum.
19 Five T-34 / 85s were captured intact and immediately reused by the Finns who registered them Ps. 245-1, 245-2, 245-3, 245-4, 245-5; the other two wagons, damaged, were transferred to the Varkaus workshop which returned them to the repaired department, registered Ps. 245-6 and 245-7, on September 1st.

▲ The only D-8 armored car (Dyrenkov-8), registered R-6, captured by the Finns and never used in combat. Behind him a B-10 (SA-kuva Archive).

▲ A BA-20 armored car captured from the Soviets and reused by the Finns (SA-kuva Archive).

▼ A BA-10 armored car used by the Finns in the Prääsä-Matrosa sector, September 1941 (www.live.warthunder.com).

▲ Finnish officer sitting on the turret of a Soviet BA-10 armored car captured on August 17, 1941 (SA-kuva Archive).

▼ Two Finnish BA-10 armored cars (SA-kuva Archive).

▲ BA-20 armored car equipped with radio, captured from the Soviets, precedes a T-26C tank during a parade (https://smolbattle.ru)

▼ A BT-5 tank reused by the Finns near Vitele in August 1941 (SA-kuva Archive).

▲ BT-5 tank, registered R-99, with infantry on board marching towards Vitele in August 1941. The officers alongside the tank are Major General Paavo Talvela and Colonel Ruben Lagus (SA-kuva Archive).

▼ Soviet light tractor T-20 "Komsomolets" used by the Finns with a towed anti-tank gun (SA-kuva archive).

▲ Soviet light tractor T-20 "Komsomolets" used by the Finns with a French 75 mm model 1897 cannon in tow (www.foto-history.livejournal.com).

▼ Maintenance of a Soviet T-20 "Komsomolets" light tractor reused by the Finnish departments (SA-kuva Archive).

▲ The Landsverk 182 armored car in the city of Petrozavodsk, note the 20 mm L-39 anti-tank rifle and the blue swastika, October 1941 (SA-kuva archive).

▼ The T-28 tank captured in Viipuri on 8 July 1941 in service in the heavy tank platoon of the Pansaaripataljioona with its crew (www.waralbum.ru).

▲ Finnish T-28 tank in Petrozavods occupied on 2 October 1941 (SA-kuva archive).

▼ Finnish tank T-28, R-48, crosses a temporary wooden bridge in Vitele on 27 August 1941 (SA-kuva archive).

▲ Two Finnish crew members pose in front of their T-28 in the spring of 1942 (www.foto-history.livejournal.com).

▼ One of the two T-28 tanks captured by the Finns in December 1939, registered R-48, was reused in the heavy tank platoon of the Pansaaripataljioona (www.waralbum.ru).

▲ A Finnish T-28 tank damaged to the left track during training (SA-kuva archive).

▼ Two T-28 tanks in service in the heavy tank platoon of the Pansaaripataljioona (SA-kuva Archive).

▲ A Finnish T-38 amphibious tank crosses a watercourse on 1 July 1942 (SA-kuva archive).

▼ A T-38 amphibious tank captured and exhibited, along with other captured vehicles, at the Finnish war booty exhibition (Sotasaalisnättely) in Helsinki in September 1941 (SA-kuva archive).

▲ A tank T-26 mod. 1931 captured and exhibited in the Finnish war booty exhibition (Sotasaalisnättely) in Helsinki in September 1941 (SA-kuva archive).

▼ The T-26A tank, registered R-83, belonging to the 3rd company in Pajatusova, in the Svir river region, used for towing refueling trucks in September 1941 (SA-kuva archive).

▲ Column of T-26C marching towards Nuosjarvi, in the Karelian Isthmus, on 11 September 1941 (SA-kuva Archive).

▼ An OT-130 flamethrower tank, reused by the Finns and registered under the number R-94, during the fighting for the conquest of Petrozavodsk on 1 October 1941 (SA-kuva archive).

▲ 3rd Company T-26E tanks ready for an attack from Tuulosjoki to Syvär in September 1941 (www.sotahistoriallisetkohte-et.fi).

▼ Tank OT-133 - 1939 model with cannonless flamethrower in Petrozavodsk on October 1, 1941 (SA-kuva Archive).

▲ A T-26C tank, accompanied by infantry, enters the village of Tuulos on 5 September 1941 (www.foto-history.livejournal.com).

▼ A T26B tank and a DKW 500 motorcycle parked towards Tuulos-Aunus, on 5 September 1941 (SA-kuva archive).

▲ Right to left: T-26B, T-26C, T-26A and two T26Es advance along with the infantry (https://panzerphotos.com/vickers-6-ton).

▼ Finnish T-26C tank Ps164-7 captured by the Soviets in June 1944 (www.foto-history.livejournal.com).

▲ Finnish Ps164-7 T-26C tank captured by the Soviets in June 1944 (www.foto-history.livejournal.com)

▲ T-26E tank belonging to the 3rd company in Tuulos in September 1941 (www.live.warthunder.com).

▼ T-26E tank used in the battle of Viipuri in June 1944 (www.live.warthunder.com).

▲ T-26E tanks advance into Karelia in December 1941 (SA-kuva archive).

▼ T-26E tank marching along the streets of Petrozavodsk on October 1, 1941 (https://smolbattle.ru).

▲ One of the two T-26T armored tractors used by the Finns for training tankers during the Continuation War (www.jaegerplatoon.net).

▼ T26T tractor used by the Finnish army in 1945 (www.jaegerplatoon.net).

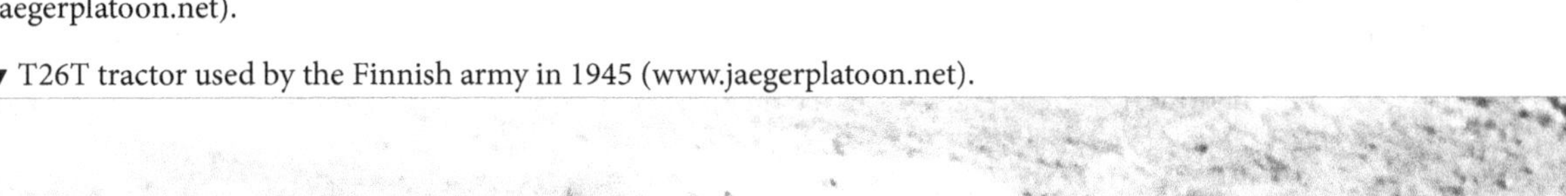

▲ T26 tank transformed by the Finns into a self-propelled prototype with 120 mm mortar (http://ftr.wot-news.com).

▼ BT-42 assault cannon destroyed at Viipuri railway station on June 20, 1944 (www.waralbum.ru).

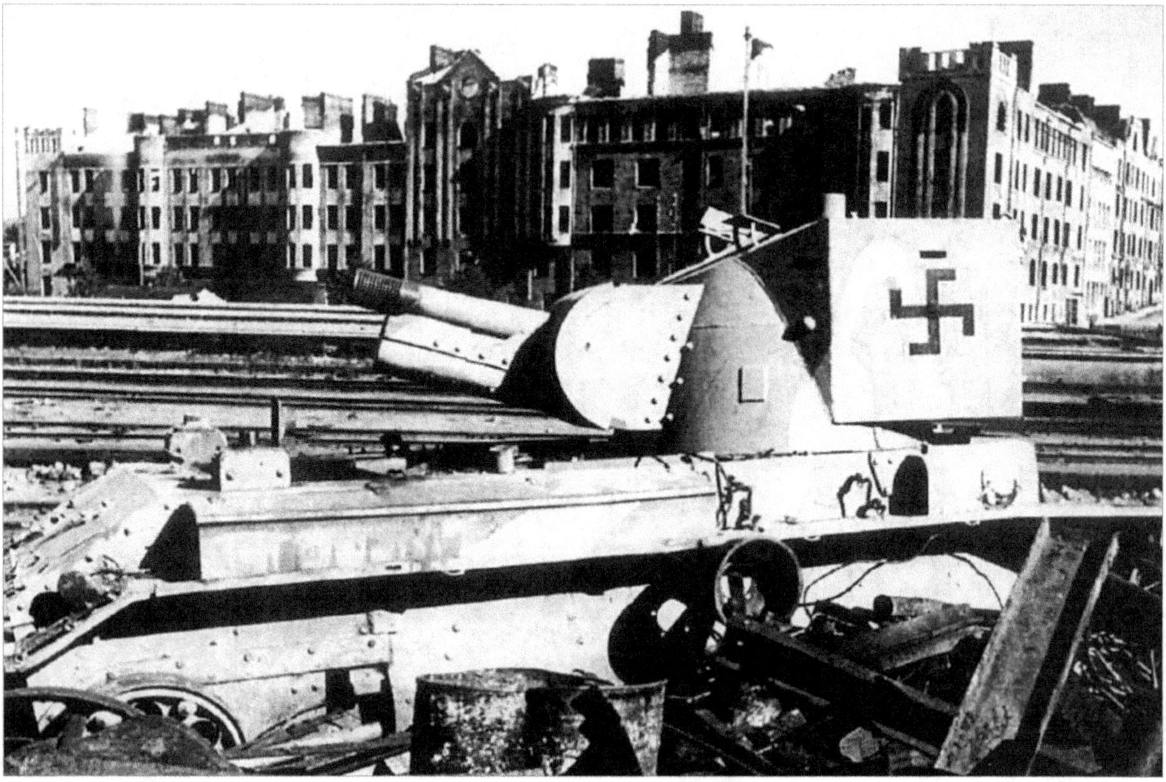

▲ A BT-42 assault cannon, registered under the number R-705, in Petrozavodsk in 1943 (www.waralbum.ru).

▼ A BT-42 assault cannon in Petrozavodsk (www.waralbum.ru).

▲ The assault cannon BT-42, R-717 of ten. Stig Sippel, destroyed in Viipuri on 20 June 1944 (www.sotahistoriallisetkohte-et.fi).

▼ Column of tanks participating in a parade in Enso before the Soviet offensive in Karelia in June 1944, left to right T-26C R-124, T-50 R-110, Landsverk Anti II R-902, BT-42, T-34 Ps.231-2 and T-28 (probably R-102 or R-103) (Archive SA-kuva).

▲ The BT-42 R-706 assault cannon in a pause in the fighting (www.vieremanveteraanit.fi).

▼ A Landsverk L-62 Anti II belonging to the self-propelled anti-aircraft battery in service in the Panssaridivisioona deployed in the Liikola region, Isthmus of Karelia 15 June 1944 (SA-kuva Archive).

▲ A Landsverk L-62 Anti II belonging to the self-propelled anti-aircraft battery in service in the Panssaridivisioona in Enso, June 4, 1944 (www.live.warthunder.com).

▼ A Landsverk L-62 Anti II during the acceptance tests conducted by the Finnish army (SA-kuva Archive).

▲ A Landsverk L-62 Anti II during a presentation of the armored vehicles to the military authorities (SA-kuva Archive).

▲ Colonel Sven Krister Björkman, commander of the Armored Battalion in 1939 and later of the Armored Brigade from May 1942 to December 1944 (www.wikidata.org).

▲ Major General Ernst Ruben Lagus, commander of the Armored Division since June 1942 (www.wikidata.org).

▲ "Laguksen Nuolet" - "Lagus Arrows", the armored division emblem representing a green triangle containing three yellow and black arrows pointing to the right, designed by Major General Lagus (www.vieremanveteraanit.fi).

▼ Stu 40 G prepare to parade in Enso on 4 June 1944 in front of Marshal Mannerheim and President Ryti. Note the modifications introduced on the vehicle by the Finns: spare routes positioned on the sides of the casemate, Soviet DT 7.62 mm machine gun, shielded position for the machine gun (SA-kuva archive).

▲ A Stu 40G marching to Tali-Ihantala in June 1944 (SA-kuva Archive).

▼ A Stu 40G near Vuosalmi in July 1944. Also on this vehicle there are the logs on the sides and the pouring of concrete on the front of the casemate to increase protection. (www.live.warthunder.com).

▲ A Stu 40 G assault cannon, registered Ps 531-34, photographed in August 1944, you can see the changes made by the Finns to improve the protection of the casemate: 3 logs placed on the sides and poured concrete on the front plate. On this Stu 40G there is also the zimmerit (SA-kuva Archive).

▼ The Stu 40G, registered Ps 531-5, awaits the order to advance towards Tienhaara on 23 June 1944 (SA-kuva Archive).

▲ The crew of the Stu 40G, registered Ps 531-8, intent on refueling ammunition in the Viipuri sector in July 1944 (SA-kuva Archive).

▼ The Stu 40 G Ps 531-42 well camouflaged during the battle of Vuosalmi. Note the concrete reinforcement and the trunks on the sides of the casemate, the DT machine gun without protective shield, the mantle of the "saukopfblende" cannon (SA-kuva archive).

▲ T-50 tank captured from the Soviets and reused by the Finnish army (SA-kuva Archive).

▼ A newly refurbished KV-1 tank in Varkaus and ready to be delivered to the army (SA-kuva archive).

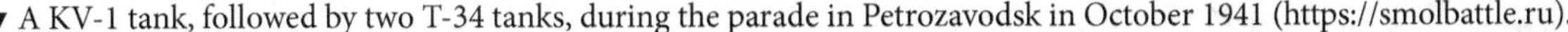

▲ One of the two KV-1 tanks captured from the Soviets and reused by the Finns in the Karelian Isthmus in July 1944 (www.live.warthunder.com).

▼ A KV-1 tank, followed by two T-34 tanks, during the parade in Petrozavodsk in October 1941 (https://smolbattle.ru).

▲ One of the two KV-1 tanks captured by the Finns used in barrage tests on 3 September 1943 (SA-kuva archive).

▲ Tank T-34/76 in service in the heavy tank platoon of the Pansaaripataljioona (SA-kuva Archive).

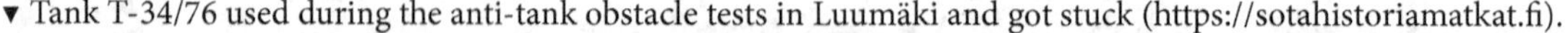

▲ One of the first Soviet T-34/76 tanks captured by the Finns during the fighting in Karelia near Medvezhyegorsk, was registered under the number R105 (www.foto-history.livejournal.com).

▼ Tank T-34/76 used during the anti-tank obstacle tests in Luumäki and got stuck (https://sotahistoriamatkat.fi).

▲ One of the T-34/85 tanks captured in the Karelian Isthmus in July 1944 and reused by the Finns (www.live.warthunder.com).

▼ A group of Finnish soldiers posing on a T-34 tank captured in Raisala in the Karelian Isthmus in August 44 (SA-kuva Archive).

▲ Tank T-34/85 in service in the Finnish units in Salo Iisakkala in August 1944 (SA-kuva Archive).

▼ One of the two ISU-152 assault guns captured by the Finns and reused (SA-kuva Archive).

▲ A BT-42 used for the recovery of a T-34 off-road around Viipuri (taken from "Vänrikki Stig Holmströmin tie Äänislinnasta Karjalan Kannakselle ja Lapin sotaan 1943-1944", S. Holmström 2016).

▼ T.20 light tractor with towed pak in the Karelian woods (SA-kuva archive).

▲   Lieutenant Sippel's BT-42 R-717 during the refueling of shells for the 114 mm howitzer in the Karelian Isthmus in June 1944 (taken from "Vänrikki Stig Holmströmin tie Äänislinnasta Karjalan Kannakselle ja Lapin sotaan 1943-1944", S . Holmström 2016).

"LAPIN SOTA" – THE LAPLAND WAR

Among the clauses of the armistice, signed in Moscow on September 19, the Soviets imposed on the Finns the withdrawal of the Germans from their territory by September 15, after that date the German troops, still present on Finnish soil, had to be disarmed, captured and surrender to them if necessary by force. Thus began the Lapland War.

In agreement with the Germans, during the first weeks the retreat of the Wehrmacht took place without particular problems, the Finnish troops attacked positions already abandoned without having to fight.

The Panssaridivisioona was sent north to join the troops already engaged against the Germans. Arrived in Oulu between 22 and 25 September, she received the order to disarm the German troops, belonging to the 7th Gebirgs-Division, present in the city of Pudasjärvi. Some T-26 tanks of the assault tank battalion and the 5th Jäger battalion were used which, upon reaching the city, were blocked by the German rearguard. They were asked to surrender by the Finnish commander, which was refused. A brief firefight then began with some losses on the German side. The Finns settled around Pudasjärvi and entered the city two days later following the retreat of the German units.

On 1 October the 1st company of the 1st Panssaripataljoona landed in Tornio with its T-26s, the only wagons that, given their size, could be transported by the available ships and unloaded from the modest port facilities present. Until 8 October the company participated in the fighting for the liberation of the city and its surroundings. During the clashes there was the last tank fight by the Finnish units, a T-26E destroyed a French Somua 35 tank in service in the Panzer-Abteilung 211, while the T-26B Ps. 163-42 was hit by a German Pak 40 which damaged the rolling train.

After the conclusion of the battle for the liberation of Tornio, the 1st company was sent to Rovaniemi, but on 21 October received the order to return to the starting base. The Lapland War for the 1st Company was over.

The 2nd and 3rd companies of the 1st Panssaripataljoona, equipped with T-34/85 and T-34/76, also took part in the Lapin Sota. Unable to be transported by sea, the companies made the transfer to the front line by land, going up north along roads in poor condition due to the numerous demolitions carried out by the retreating Germans. On the route from Oulu to Sodankylä, crossing Pudasjärvi - Ranua - Rovaniemi, the number of operational T-34s gradually decreased due to breakdowns affecting numerous wagons. After Pudasjärvi, due to the wooded and rough terrain not suitable for the use of armored vehicles, the wagons were used only for the transport of supplies and the evacuation of the wounded from the front.

Between 12 and 16 October the armored units of the Panssaridivisioona participated in the reconquest of the city of Rovaniemi, with very violent clashes that destroyed about 90% of the buildings. It was the last battle fought by the divisions of the Division.

The last three T-34/76 tanks in service in the 3rd Company advanced up to 159 km north of Rovaniemi, when they were blocked by mechanical problems. The T-34/85 of the 3rd company, after passing Sodankylä, were stopped and received the order to return to the base.

During the operational cycle carried out during the Lapland War, the two T-34 companies were never involved in clashes with the German armored forces, only the T-34/76 231-6 was seriously damaged by a German anti-tank mine, but he was then repaired by continuing his service in the Finnish army.

The two mixed companies Pz.Kw IVJ / Stu 40G of the 2nd Panssaripataljoona also participated in the War of Lapland, but never had the opportunity to clash with the German troops, returning to their starting base at the end of October. On 20 September at the PzKw IVJ 231-4 the engine caught fire, despite the prompt intervention of the tankers, the damage was significant and the tank was declared unrepairable and removed from the inventory.

The armistice clauses also included the one that provided for the demobilization of a large part of the Finnish armed forces, including the Panssaridivisioona.

The Panssaridivisioona was withdrawn from the front at the end of October and placed in reserve. On November 21, 1944, the armored component of the division was reduced to a single battalion and the wagons in service were stored in the Parola depot.

On 30 December 1944 the Panssaridivisioona was dissolved.

Thus ended, with the dissolution, the brief operational activity, lasting less than thirty months, of the only Armored Division in service in the Suomen Maavoimat, an activity that had cost the sacrifice of a total of 4,308 soldiers. Despite the short period of activity, the Finnish tankers demonstrated their professionalism in the field, using obsolete means at best and not at the level of those used by the enemy, receiving praise for their combativeness from the ally and the enemy.

It should be noted that, from the beginning of the Continuation War to the end of the Lapland War, despite the numerous battles sustained, no T-28s and no T-34s were lost, some were damaged, even with human losses, but they were always repaired and returned to fight against their previous owners.

As of January 1, 1945, the Finnish army had in charge the following vehicles between armored and armored vehicles: 15 BA-20, 3 FAI, 12 BA-10, 10 BA-6, 1 BA-3, 19 (according to other sources 23) T-26E, 82 T-26 (all variants including tractors), 1 T-50, 2 KV-1, 7 T-28[20], 9 T-34/76 [21], 9 T-34/85[22], 6 Landsverk Anti II, 3 T-38, 9 T-38/34, 3 T-38/KV, 1 tractor on chassis ISU-152, 14 PzKw IVJ, 47 StuG-40[23], 10 BT-42, 1 BT-43, 134 T-20 "Komsomolets".

---

20 Not having in service rescue vehicles suitable for the recovery of medium and / or heavy tanks, in September 1944 it was decided to transform the T-28E R-104 into an armored rescue vehicle. After the modification it was registered as T-28V Ps.735-1. All the T-28s, including the T-28V, were only sold on November 30, 1951, at least 3 still exist in some museums.

21 In addition to the 7 T-34 / 76s in service, of which 4 captured from the Soviets and 3 purchased by the Germans, two other T-34s were captured by the Finns in the summer of 1944. They were probably never repaired but used as sources of parts of spare parts, however they were supplied and regularly inventoried. The last T-34 / 76s are alienated at the end of 1961. To date, 5 examples survive in museums or barracks.

22 There were 7 T-34 / 85s in service in the Finnish units, but two other tanks were captured by the Soviets: one in Portinhoikka between 25 and 26 June 1944 and the other in Vuosalmi on 31 August. They are regularly inventoried but not assigned to the departments. The T-34/85 captured in Vuosalmi was registered Ps.245-9. The last T-34 / 85s were alienated in September 1962. To date, 5 examples survive in museums or barracks.

23 There were 8 Stug 40Gs lost in the fighting, but due to the lack of spare parts not purchased together with the vehicles, it was forced to cannibalize some assault guns to recover the materials needed to carry out repairs on the other vehicles. Stu 40G were thus cannibalized: Ps.531-13 in the year 1943 and Ps.531-7, Ps.531-28 and Ps.531-53 subsequently, which were removed from the inventory of equipment supplied in October 1944. From the 59 assault guns delivered, the number of 47 supplied at the end of 1944 was reached. They remained in service until 1959.

▲ PzKw IVJ tank, registered Ps. 221-1, of the 2nd Armored Battalion at the Oulu bridge on 11 December 1944 (SA-kuva Archive).

▼ PzKw IVJ tank, registered Ps. 221-6, of the 2nd armored battalion at the Oulu bridge on 11 December 1944 (SA-kuva Archive).

▲ KV-1 Ps 272-1 tank used during the Lapland War in late 1944 (www.waralbum.ru).

▼ T-26B tank at Tornio in October 1944 (www.sotahistoriallisetkohteet.fi).

▲ T26-C tank marching to Rovaniemi on October 16, 1944 (http://tankfront.ru/finland).

▼ Stu 40 G assault cannon, registered Ps 531-40, used during the war in Lapland (www.picuki.com).

▲ Stu 40 G assault cannon, registered Ps 531-45, used during the war in Lapland (www.picuki.com).

▼ French Somua S35 tank, in service in the German Panzer-Abteilung 211, destroyed by the Finnish T26s during the battle of Tornio in October 1944 (SA-kuva Archive).

CAMOUFLAGE, INSIGNIA, REGISTRATION NUMBER

At the beginning of the Winter War, Finnish tanks were painted with the dark green color, in 1943, during the Continuation War, a three-tone camouflage scheme was introduced: moss green - sand brown - light gray. The self-propelled anti-aircraft Landswerk Anti II remained colored with the original Swedish factory camouflage: gray-green - brown - yellow brown. In winter the vehicles were camouflaged with white paint, in some cases totally in others only with stripes of color.

During the Winter War, a blue and white striped band was painted around the turrets of the Vickers 6-Ton tanks as an identifying mark to distinguish the vehicle from similar Soviet tanks. From June 1941, all vehicles began to be marked with the new national symbol: the Hakaristas. Following the armistice with the Soviet Union in 1944, a round blue and white rosette with a diameter of 240 or 300 mm was adopted in 1945 instead of the Hakaristi. The Hakaristas, 32 centimeters tall and black and white, had to be 3 in the middle and positioned on both sides and back of the turret. In 1943 two more Hakaristas were added, on the front of the vehicle and on the top, or on the hatch, of the turret. Some autonomous departments equipped with armored bus vehicles had the Hakaristi in blue or even white.

During the Winter War, no tactical symbols were used on the tanks of the Panssaripataljoona, while with the start of the Continuation War, white or yellow symbols were painted on the front of the front to identify the three companies:

- 1st company: Bear's head
- 2nd company: Flying Dragon
- 3rd company: Death's head

With the establishment of the Panssariprikaati in 1942, new tactical symbols were adopted to identify the vehicles in service in the two battalions.

The three companies of the 1st Panssaripataljoona adopted white geometric figures, inside which a Roman numeral was inserted indicating the position of the chariot within its platoon. The chariots with numbers from 1 to 5 belonged to the 1st Platoon, those from 6 to 10 to the 2nd and those from 11 to 15 the 3rd. The tanks with the number 0 were those of the company commander.

- 1st company: Square
- 2nd company: Circle
- 3rd company: Triangleo

The three companies of the 2nd Panssaripataljoona instead adopted a system of fractional numbers, white in color for all companies. The chariots of the company commanders were numbered 1/4, 1/5, 1/6, while within the platoons the numbering was as follows:

- 1st platoon: 1 / I to 5 / I
- 2nd platoon: 1 / II to 5 / II
- 3rd platoon: 1 / III to 5 / III

From mid-1943 the German three-number system was adopted, which used colors to diversify companies and numbers to identify company, platoon and tank. However, this system was not very widespread among the departments, even if it is used.

All Finnish tanks and armored cars, until 1943, were registered using a Rekisterinumero (registration number) painted in white on the front of the vehicle. The vehicles were then registered as R followed by a progressive number, for example R-77 was a T-26, R-712 a BT-42, regardless of the type of vehicle and the date of entry into service. In 1943 a new registration system was adopted, which consisted of the designator Panssarivaunu (tank) Ps. followed by a one to three digit number indicating the vehicle model type and a further one to three digit number indicating the individual vehicle number. This numbering was in white letters and, as a rule, was applied to the front and back of the vehicles. A T-26 was therefore registered, for example, as: Ps. 162-9; a PzKw IVJ: Ps. 261-11.

The following three-digit numbers were used to indicate the models of the following tanks and assault guns:

- T-26: according to model 161 - 162 - 163 - 164
- T-34/76: 231
- T-34/85: 245
- T-28: 241
- KV-1 model 1942: 271-1
- KV-1E model 1940: 272-1
- BT-5: 176
- BT-42: 511
- BT-43: 611-1
- Stu 40G: 531
- PzKw IVJ: 221

The armored cars in service in the Finnish departments were instead numbered with the following numbers:

- BA-3: 25
- BA-6: 26
- BA-10: 27
- FAI: 5
- FAI M - BA-20 - BA-20M: 6

However, the new numbering was not fully applied, in fact many BT-42 tanks and assault guns kept the old Rekisterinumero registration throughout the Continuation War.

▲ Platoon of Pzkw IVJ headed to Oulu station on 12 November 1944 (SA-kuva Archive).

▲ The T-28 R-102 during the offensive for the conquest of Povenetz (SA-kuva Archive).

▼ Armored car BA-10 captured intact from the Soviets in September 1941 (SA-kuva Archive).

▲ The T-34/76 Ps.231-2, followed by the T-28 R-102 or R.103, during the parade at Enso on June 4, 1944 (SA-kuva Archive).

▼ The newly repaired T-50 at the Varkaus workshop in January 1942 (SA-kuva Archive).

▲ Four T.28 and T.34 during the parade of units in the city of Petrozavodsk in October 1942 (SA-kuva Archive)

▼ A group of officers of the Panssaridivisioona in May 1944, from left: Lieutenant Hellamo, Captain Troil, Major General Lagus, Colonel Björkman and Lieutenant Godenceutz.

▲ T-26C R-99 intent on recovering a T-26B stuck in a channel (www.missing-lynx.com).

▼ T 26A R-78 (T-26 model 1931) at Aunus/Olonets after the capture of the town in September 1941 (SA-kuva Archive).

BIBLIOGRAPHY

Books

- Saurio J., "Hyökkäysvaunurykmentinperustamisesta 100 vuotta", 2019.
- Holmströmin S., "Erillinen panssarikomppania 1943-1944", 2016.
- Häkkinen S., "Sauli Häkkinen in guerra 18 anni - 23 anni", 2017.
- Longo Adorno M., "La guerra d'inverno: Finlandia e Unione Sovietica, 1939-1940", Franco Angeli, 2010.
- Petacco A. – "Le grandi battaglie del Ventesimo Secolo" - Curcio Editore – 1982.

Magazines

- Rossotto R., "1917-1919: la Finlandia dall'indipendenza alla guerra", in "Storia Militare", numbers 291/292.
- "Storia Illustrata", various numbers.
- "Eserciti & Armi", various numbers.

Web sites

- www.SA-kuva.fi
- www.waralbum.ru
- www.jaegerplatoon.net
- https://it.topwar.ru
- www:yle.fi
- www.hameensanomat.fi
- www.andreaslarka.net
- www.vieremanveteraanit.fi
- www.foto-history.livejournal.com
- www.smolbattle.ru
- www.sotahistoriallisetkohteet.fi
- www.picuki.com
- https://panzerphotos.com/vickers-6-ton
- www.palasuomenhistoriaa.net
- www.suomensotilas.fi
- www.live.warthunder.com

TITOLI GIÀ PUBBLICATI
TITLES ALREADY PUBLISHING

BOOKS TO COLLECT